beautiful **boxes**

beautiful boxes

Clarkson N. Potter, Inc./Publishers

CONTENTS

1

Papercrafts

2

Découpage

3

Paint effects

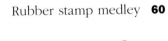

4
Natural choice

5
Fabulous fabric

6
Design in 3-D

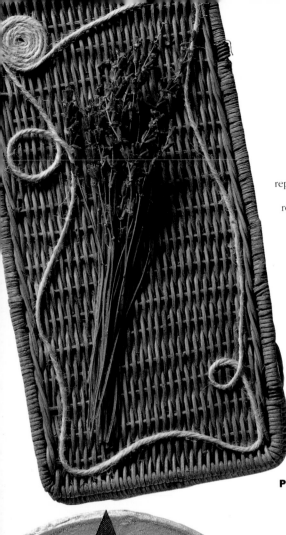

A QUARTO BOOK

Published by Clarkson N. Potter, Inc.,
201 East 50th Street, New York, New York 10022.
Member of the Crown Publishing Group.

Random House, Inc. New York, Toronto, London,
Sydney, Auckland

CLARKSON N. POTTER, POTTER, and colophon
are trademarks of Clarkson N. Potter, Inc.

This book was designed and produced by
Quarto Publishing plc
6 Blundell Street
London N7 9BH

Senior Art Editor Toni Toma
Designer John Grain
Senior Editor Eileen Cadman
Text Editor Barbara Cheney
Photography Martin Norris, Les Weis, Laura Wickenden
Editorial Director Mark Dartford
Art Director Moira Clinch

Manufactured by Regent Publishing Services Ltd,
Hong Kong
Printed by Leefung-Asco Printers Ltd, China

Library of Congress Cataloging-in-Publication Data
is available on request.

ISBN 0-517-88624-3

10 9 8 7 6 5 4 3 2 1
First American Edition

Introduction

Much of the fun of decorating boxes is in revamping old boxes that have seen better days. It is surprisingly simple to make new, designer-style containers very economically. Use your creations to store jewelry, needlework tools, photographs, and letters, or to hide a special gift. All of the boxes make lovely gifts themselves.

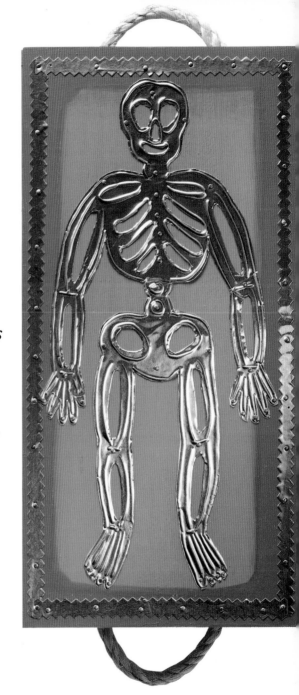

Equipment

You probably already possess most of the basic equipment needed to decorate boxes. Always work on a clean, flat surface, and keep sharp implements, paints, and glues beyond the reach of children.

Drawing tools

Use an HB pencil for drawing. Keep pencils sharp-pointed for accuracy or use a propeling pencil. Always use a ruler and set square when drawing squares and rectangles so that the angles are accurate. Use a compass to draw circles.

Cutting tools

Sharp pointed scissors are the most versatile for craftwork. Choose a pair that feels comfortable. For cutting detailed shapes, a small pair is best. For découpage, embroidery or manicure scissors are more suitable. Curved manicure scissors are useful for cutting curves. Use dressmaking scissors for cutting fabric, but not to cut paper as it will blunt the blades. Embroidery scissors are best for intricate fabric motifs and threads.

Craft knives and scalpels make a neat cut on paper and cardboard. Always use them on a cutting mat and replace the blades frequently, as a blunt blade will tear paper. Do not use a craft knife to cut tissue paper as it will rip. Cut straight edges against a metal ruler. Use wire cutters or an old pair of scissors to cut metals.

Adhesives

The large variety of materials that can be used to decorate boxes means that more than one type of glue may be needed for a project. Always follow the manufacturer's instructions carefully and test first on any scraps. To distribute the glue evenly, use a plastic spreader or thin strip of cardboard. For intricate areas use a cocktail stick.

PVA (polyvinyl acetate) medium is a very versatile craft glue. It is a non-toxic white solution

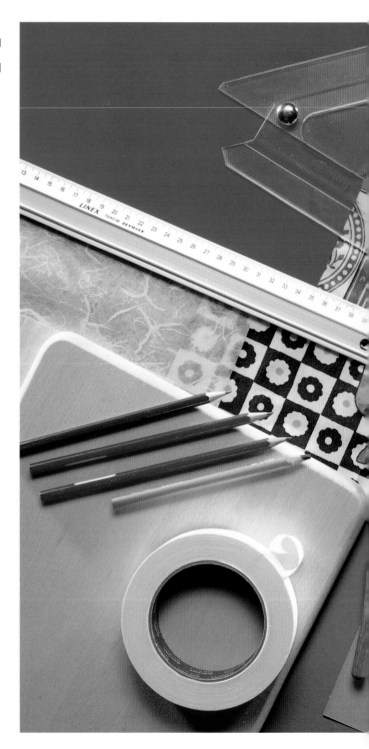

that dries clear. Use it for gluing paper and fabric and for making papier-mâché models.

Superglue (strong epoxy resin) is very strong and will stick paper, cardboard, metal, wood, fabric, and some plastics. Always handle superglue carefully: a gel glue is easier to apply than the liquid form if you need only a small amount. Store superglue upright to prevent clogging.

All-purpose household glue and rubber glue are both suitable for gluing materials such as paper, cardboard, beads, and pressed flowers. If you plan to do a lot of craftwork, buy a glue gun. It is quick and easy to use and suitable for many materials.

Painting tools

For best results use the paintbrush recommended for the type of paint that you are using. Good-quality artist's brushes are worth the expense. Use a fine paintbrush for detailed work. Always clean brushes well immediately after use. Use a stenciling brush for stenciling.

Paint can also be applied with a sponge or spattered with an old toothbrush for random speckled effects. A badger-hair varnishing brush is best for applying varnish, but a flat paintbrush would also be suitable.

Materials

Choosing boxes

Choosing a suitable box to decorate needs a little thought. For example, what is the purpose of the box? Will it have a practical use for storage, or is it to be purely decorative? Do you intend it as a gift for someone? What should it be made of? A box for storing stationery or toys may need to be hardwearing, so would metal or wood be the best material? Jewelry boxes are handled more carefully, so a variety of materials could be used. Purely ornamental boxes can be delicate or hard-wearing.

Look out for interesting boxes at junk shops or revitalize old seed boxes and shoeboxes. Plain cardboard and wooden box "blanks" are available from craft stores ready for decoration.

The box needs to be suited to its proposed decoration. Be sure that a lid that slips over the top of the box will still fit once it has been covered with paper, fabric, or paint. The lid of a wooden box can be sanded inside to make it fit.

Preparation

Secondhand boxes may need some preparation first. Sandpaper wooden boxes to even out the surface and to prepare for painting. Fill any cracks with wood filler, let dry, then sand down.

To prepare a metal or enamel box, clean off any rust with a wire brush and wet-and-dry paper, then apply a coat of metal primer.

Paper and cardboard

There is a huge choice of paper available. Giftwrap paper is an inexpensive way of transforming a plain box. Even corrugated cardboard can be used creatively. Art stores and specialty paper stores stock some beautiful examples such as wood veneer papers, textured, and handmade papers which, although expensive, will make a simple project very special.

Stencil board has a waxed coating which means that it can be re-used. Stencils can also be cut from

acetate or cardboard. Mat board is made of layers of compressed paper. It must be cut with a craft knife. Use mat board to add three-dimensional details.

Paints

Boxes to be painted may need undercoat. Use acrylic gesso or emulsion paint for water-based paints and an oil-based primer for oil-based paints.

Craft paints are very versatile and come in a wide choice of finishes. Acrylic and poster paints are available in a large range of colors.

Although oil paints are slow-drying, the result is worth waiting for. India inks give interesting translucent effects. Puff and glitter paints come in bottles with a thin nozzle to apply the paint which dries slightly embossed. Metallic powders can be rubbed into wood or clay to color the surface.

Spray paints give an even covering of paint and can be used for stenciling.

Natural materials

The back yard can provide a wonderful choice of materials to use for decorating boxes.

The seashore is another great source of exciting natural materials. Shells, driftwood, and sea-smoothed pebbles work well together. Specialty shell stores sell exotic shells and accessories.

Raffia can be woven or tied to create ethnic styles. Both natural and dyed shades can be bought. Raffia, string, and cord can be dyed with fabric dyes.

Needlework materials

Beautiful fabrics will transform a plain box very quickly. As only small amounts of fabric are needed, search offcuts and remnants at fabric stores.

Modeling materials

Stylish boxes can be made from scratch using fine metal foil or decorated with motifs modeled from clay. Air-drying clay is simple to use and can be painted.

Polymer clay is available in many colors, it is hardened by baking in an oven for a short time. Papier mâché pulp can be bought in dry form that is then mixed with water, or it can be made by hand.

Salt dough is now enjoying a welcome revival. Made from flour, salt, and water, the dough is baked slowly in a cool oven. It can then be painted. Varnished well and kept away from moisture it can last for years.

La lune blanche
Luit dans les bois;
De chaque branche
Part une voix
Sous la ramée...
Ô bien-aimée.

L'étang reflète,
Profond miroir,
La silhouette
Du saule noir
Où le vent pleure...
Rêvons: c'est l'heure.

Verlaine

Papercrafts

Papercrafts are a good starting point, as paper and cardboard are some of the most economical materials.

Glue on cut or torn colored papers. Recycle newspapers to make papier-mâché pulp and mold into unusual sculptural motifs.

Marquetry **magic**

This is an inexpensive version of the beautiful wood craft of marquetry. Wood veneer papers are cut and glued to resemble fine inlaid wood.

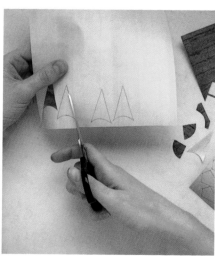

1 With a pencil, draw around the box lid on tracing paper and cut out. Draw a simple design such as this nautical compass within the circumference. Place the tracing face down on the wrong side of one of the papers and secure in place with masking tape. Check that the wood grain is lying in a suitable direction then trace the outline to transfer it. Use a ruler for straight lines.

2 In this way, transfer each section of the design to the papers; then carefully cut them out.

3 Tape the tracing right side up at one edge of the lid. Using a paintbrush, apply white glue to the paper sections and glue them to the lid. Work out from the center and slip each piece under the tracing to help with correct positioning. Add a coordinating border around the rim if you wish. Coat with varnish if the box is to be handled often.

Safari stripes

Torn strips of leatherette paper are applied to a cardboard box to achieve this stunning zebra-skin effect. Experiment with other color combinations to make tiger and leopard-skin boxes.

You **will need . . .**

- Cardboard box
- Black and white leatherette paper
- Scissors
- White glue
- Flat paintbrush

1 The lid: cut white leatherette paper into wavy and curved strips ⅜–¾in (1–2cm) wide. Cut the ends of the strips to a rounded point. Using a paintbrush, apply white glue to a section of the lid and stick on a strip. Apply more glue and continue to cover the lid, overlapping the strips.

2 Cover the box in the same way. Snip the excess paper at the corners. Glue paper to the inside of the box and under it as well.

3 Cut wavy and curved strips of black leatherette paper as in step 1. Apply white glue to a section of the box and glue on a black strip. Apply more strips using the same method to create a random design. Decorate the other sides and the lid in the same way. Let dry.

Cactus pencil box

This fun pencil box is a good project to do with a child. You can buy ready-made papier-mâché pulp very cheaply. It can be used in many creative ways.

You **will need . . .**

- Cardboard box with lid
- Medium-weight cardboard
- Scissors
- White glue
- Paintbrush
- Papier-mâché pulp
- Craft knife
- White latex paint
- Paintbrush
- Poster paint in shades of green
- Puff paint
- Spray varnish

1 Cut out a cactus shape in cardboard. Use a paintbrush to apply white glue to the cardboard and use papier-mâché pulp to mold the cactus shape on both sides. Smooth the edges with finger and thumb. Let it dry.

2 Cut a slit in the lid and insert the cactus. Secure it in place with extra pulp. Make small cone shapes. Dab glue around the edge of the lid and attach them. Let them dry.

3 Apply a coat of latex paint to the box and lid and leave to dry. If necessary, apply a second coat.

4 Use a paintbrush to apply green poster paint to lid, box, and cactus. Decorate cactus and cones with puff paint – this is easy to use and gives a good three-dimensional effect. When dry, spray with varnish.

Checkered tissue

Revamp a cardboard shoe box inexpensively by covering it with colorful tissue papers. Copy the checkered pattern shown here, or apply torn tissue shapes such as dots or hearts.

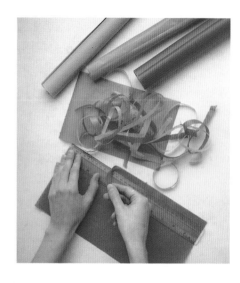

2 Completely cover the lid and box inside and out with the background-color tissue paper. Overlap the strip edges and glue the excess tissue to the underside.

You **will need . . .**

- Shoe box
- Colored tissue paper
- Ruler
- White glue
- Flat paintbrush

1 Use a light-colored tissue paper for the background. Tear into ⅜–2in (1–5cm) strips. Apply white glue to the lid. Apply a strip. Smooth out. Brush with glue.

3 Brush a line of white glue down the center of the lid and lay two colored tissue paper strips side by side. Add another pair of "stripes" equidistant and parallel to the central stripes in the same way.

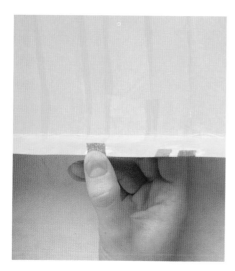

4 Glue the stripes to the sides of the lid, cut off the excess ⅜in (1cm) beyond the lid edges and glue them to the inside. Brush with glue to secure in place.

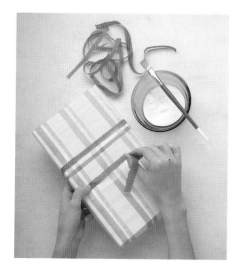

5 Apply pairs of colored strips at right angles to the stripes to make a plaid pattern. Tear squares of tissue paper and apply to each square of the plaid.

Weaving spells

Strips of painted cardboard are woven into a box and lid. The weave creates an effective broken pattern from the original painted design.

You **will need . . .**

- Cardboard – up to ¹⁄₁₆in (1mm) thick
- Acrylic paint in various colors
- Paintbrush
- Scissors
- Craft knife
- Blunt knife
- Clear varnish

To prepare the cardboard, measure and mark a 12½in (32cm) square. Use a paintbrush and bright acrylic colors to decorate both sides. Let it dry.

1 To make the lid, cut the cardboard into 16 strips ¾in (2cm) wide. Take 12 of the strips and weave six strips over and under the other six. Tighten the weave so that it leaves a solid square.

2 To make bending the strips easier, use a craft knife to very lightly score the edge of the woven square. Bend the scored strips upright.

3 To make the sides of the lid, use the remaining four strips. Thread them in and out of the upright strips. Finish the ends in the middle of an inward-facing strip.

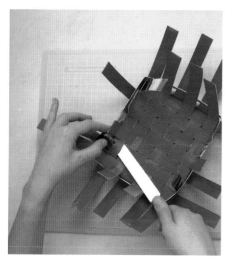

4 To finish the upright strips, measure ¾in (2cm) from the base and score. Bend the strips alternately in and out. Measure another ¾in (2cm) and score. Measure ⅜in (1cm) and cut. Bend each one over the side strip. Tuck it in using a blunt knife.

For the base, follow steps 1–4, but cut the strips ⅝in (1.5cm) wide so the base will fit the lid. To make the base deeper, weave in three side strips. Apply varnish to the box and lid.

Child's
elebox

This brightly colored box is an easy project to make with children's help. The cardboard elephant on top of the box is for holding pencils and other stationery items.

You **will need . . .**

- Hat or shoe box
- Pencil
- Scissors
- Medium-grit sandpaper
- Spray paint/poster paint in green and turquoise
- Brightly colored paper
- White glue
- Paintbrush
- Yellow puff paint
- Paper ribbon or twisted tissue
- Cardboard
- Spray varnish

1 Mark and cut a wavy edge on the lid. Sandpaper rough edges. Paint the lid and box in different colors. Cut or tear colored paper spots and triangles and glue them to the sides of the lid.

2 Make a simple elephant template. Cut out enough colored shapes to go around the box, plus two for the lid. Decorate each one with colored papers. Use puff paint for details.

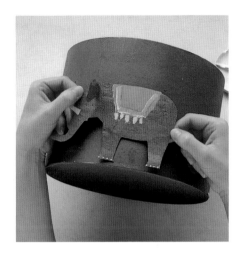

3 Glue the elephants evenly around the box. Make tails from twisted paper ribbon. Join them to the trunk of the elephant behind.

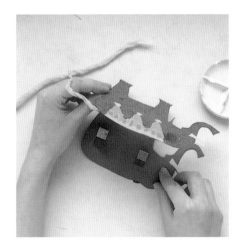

4 Mount two elephants on thin cardboard. Cut out. To glue them together: cut four small equal rectangles of cardboard. Fold each into three equal sections. Glue two pieces to the back of the body. Position the other two on the feet so they can be stuck to the lid. Glue them together and upright on the lid. Varnish.

Alphabet **set**

Dry-letter transfers come in many different scripts, colors, and sizes, and make it possible to create a box such as this very easily.

You **will need . . .**

- Wooden box with lid
- White primer paint
- Flat, fine, square-tipped paintbrush
- Fine sandpaper
- White and yellow enamel paint
- Pencil
- Clear varnish
- 4 sheets of dry-letter transfer (Letraset black and gold Palace Script was used here)

1 Paint white primer onto the box. Sand the box until it feels smooth.

2 Using the paintbrush, evenly cover the box with enamel paint. Use white with a dash of yellow. Give the box two coats, sanding between each one. An even coat is achieved by not loading the brush too heavily with paint. Make sure the brushmarks all go the same way.

3 Rub the dry-letter transfer using a pencil on the reverse side. Use the markers on the sheet to keep the spacing even. Carefully paint clear varnish over the box. Dry-letter transfer can be quite delicate, so use a fine brush.

Découpage

Découpage is a traditional craft. Paper motifs are cut out and glued to a smooth surface. Many coats of varnish are then applied to give the effect of inlay. Use printed papers, and experiment with fabric, candy wrappers, and even fine metals.

Fabric découpage

Fabric is an interesting alternative material to paper for découpage work, especially on woven surfaces such as this bamboo box.

You **will need . . .**

- Bamboo, basketry, or wicker box
- Upholstery fabric with motifs
- Plastic shopping bag
- Scissors
- White glue
- Flat paintbrush
- Polyurethane satin varnish

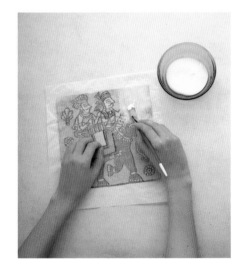

1 Cut open a plastic shopping bag to use as a protective surface. Choose a large motif on the fabric that will fit on the box lid and select smaller ones to fit on the sides. Cut them out approximately. Using a paintbrush, coat the back of the fabric with glue to help prevent fraying. Set aside to dry.

2 Cut out motifs and brush the backs with white glue. Glue the large motif on top of the lid, and the smaller motifs to the sides. Let them dry.

3 Using a paintbrush, apply six coats of polyurethane varnish, allowing each coat to dry before applying the next. The varnish will protect the box and seal the motifs.

1 Using a paintbrush, apply blue latex paint to all surfaces of the box. Let it dry and apply a second coat.

2 Mix the wallpaper paste. Cut the paper lace into sections to fit the six edges of the lid. Use your fingers to apply paste to the box edges and to the back of the paper lace. Place each section on the lid and smooth the overlapping areas.

Découpage in flower

There are many possibilities for the simple technique of découpage to decorate boxes. Here, a Victorian motif is enhanced by the texture of paper lace.

You will need . . .

- Hexagonal cardboard box with separate lid
- Blue latex paint
- Paintbrush
- Wallpaper paste
- 1 yard (1m) paper lace
- Small scissors
- Victorian "scrap" of flowers for center motif
- Clear acrylic satin varnish
- Varnish brush

3 Cut out a motif for the center and use the wallpaper paste to glue it in place. Smooth carefully with your fingers and let it dry.

4 Cut a strip of paper lace in half lengthwise and apply with paste. Align the straight edge with the base of the box, and smooth carefully.

5 When dry, apply three coats of acrylic varnish, allowing each coat to dry before applying the next.

Bowtie box

You will need ...

- Wooden box with lid
- Sandpaper
- Black acrylic paint
- Bowtie paper shapes
- Scissors
- Découpage glue
- Paintbrush

A simple stylish box for Father's Day, Christmas, or as a birthday present. It's a fun project for children to make. You can vary the decoration endlessly. The finished box is sure to be original and eye-catching.

1 Sand the box lid and base with fine sandpaper and paint with black acrylic paint. Cut out bowtie shapes (or make your own).

2 Paste a light film of découpage glue onto the back of the cutouts. With your fingers, smooth the shapes onto the box. Smooth out any bubbles and along the edges.

3 Using a paintbrush, coat the paper and box lid with découpage glue to give a flat finish. Let them dry. A second coat can be applied if desired. Brush the base of the box with glue and let it dry.

Garden **collage**

Engraved roses on wrapping paper, photocopies of wood engravings from books, and color illustrations of flowers are all used here. Antique and crackle varnishes are used to age the box.

1 Select the material and cut out, using a craft knife for fine detail.

2 Arrange the pieces into a collage on the box and glue them into place.

3 Apply aging or antique varnish to darken the material. Follow the crackle varnish manufacturer's instructions to apply the crackle varnish.

World in a box

Reproduction maps are readily obtained from museums and specialty map stores. A terrestial map was used here, but a map of the night sky would also be very effective.

1 Use the ruler and pencil to measure the box and mark your map to cover it. Cut out the map. Glue the map piece in place; make sure the edges are neat.

2 If your map is on absorbent paper, give it a coat of clear varnish. Then apply the oil-based aging varnish. Apply the crackle varnish when the aging varnish is almost dry. The surface should be dry enough for your finger to run lightly over it, yet feel sticky if you press lightly down.

3 Let the box to dry in a warm room. Use a hairdryer if cracks have not appeared, but be careful not to overheat the box since this will lift off the crackle layer.

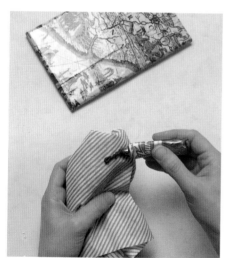

4 Once the surface is dry, rub sepia artist's oil paint into the cracks with a soft cloth. Rub very gently using a circular motion. Using a clean cloth, rub away the excess oil paint. Protect the surface with a coat of clear, oil-based varnish.

Stamps galore

Stamps are ready-made shapes to work with, and decorating this box is a good way of using up old ones. Be inventive with the patterns you make.

1 Sort the stamps according to color. Before applying any glue, experiment with arranging the stamps into a variety of patterns. Arrange a selection into a rosette shape, sticking them lightly together so that other contrasting stamps can be slipped in behind as a background.

2 When you are satisfied with the design, glue the stamps in position on the box. Use a paintbrush to apply an even coat of antique varnish.

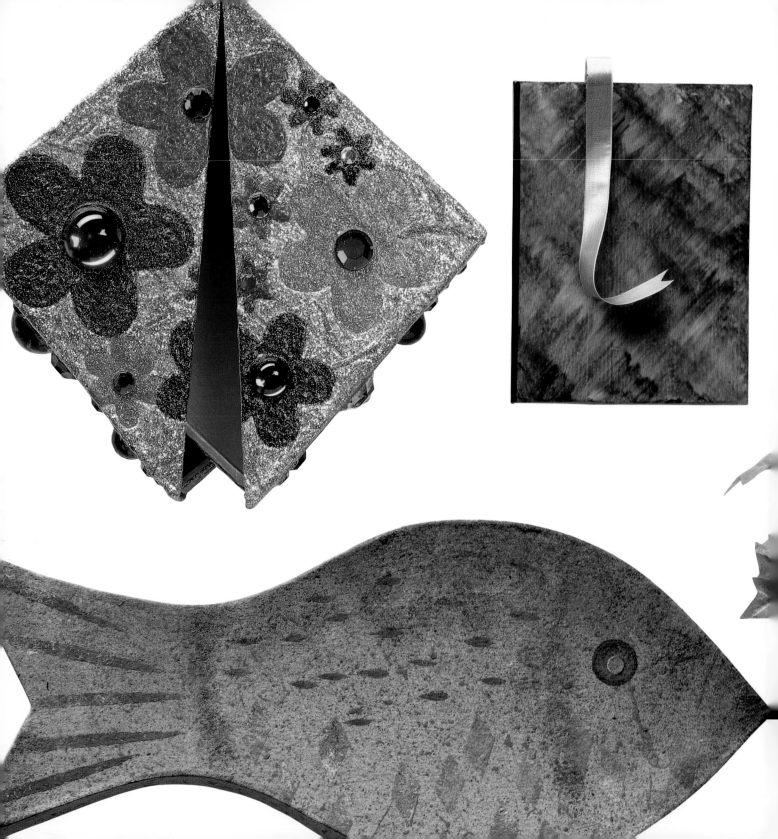

3

Paint effects

Nowadays, traditional paint techniques such as tortoiseshell and verdigris are within anyone's reach, while stenciling and stamping are ideal for the nervous painter, as professional results are easy to achieve.

1 Paint an orange border around the sides and ends of the box. Paint an orange panel on the lid, leaving a border. Paint this border and the central panels on the box pink. Let it dry.

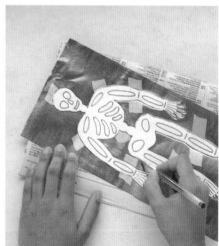

2 Make a simple skeleton template. Lay it on a piece of metal foil, secure with tape, and draw around it with a dry ballpoint pen. Draw the parts to be cut away on the template.

Day of
the dead

The Mexican Day of the Dead is based on the belief that the dead can visit their old homes without being seen by the living, and recreations of skulls and skeletons play an important role in the festivities.

You **will need . . .**

- Rectangular wooden box with lid
- Acrylic paints in bright orange and bright pink
- Paintbrush
- Skeleton template
- Aluminum foil .004 gauge 24 x 6in (60 x 15cm)
- Tape
- Dry ballpoint pen
- Small pointed scissors
- Awl
- ⅜in (1cm) brass-headed escutcheon pins
- Tackhammer
- Pinking shears

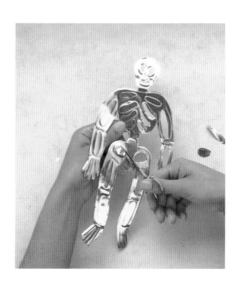

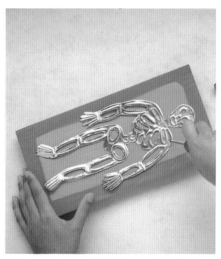

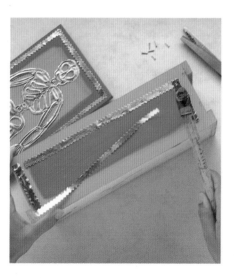

3 Remove the template. Cut out the skeleton shape and the sections in between the "ribs" and "bones." Draw lines to mark the fingers and toes.

4 Center the skeleton on the lid. Using an awl, mark holes through the foil into the metal. Using a tackhammer, tap in escutcheon pins to secure the skeleton to the lid.

5 Cut strips of foil ⅜in (1cm) wide using pinking shears. Use escutcheon pins to secure the strips around the skeleton. In the same way, attach strips on each side of the box as shown.

Lovely lace

This pretty gift box is ideal for presenting a special gift. The delicate filigree effect is created by spray-painting through paper doilys. The box is fastened with a double bow of golden ribbons.

You will need . . .

- White oval box with separate lid
- Paper doilys
- Scissors
- Spray glue
- Gold spray paint
- Newspaper
- Lighter fluid
- Soft cloth
- Gold wire-edged ribbon

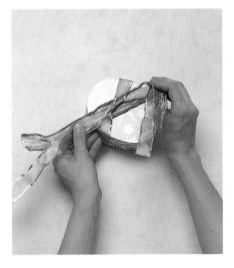

1 Use the lid as a template to cut an oval from the center of a doily. Applying the glue sparingly, glue it to the lid. Cut the rest of the doily into sections. Glue them lightly to the sides of the lid. Cut sections from doilys and glue them to the sides of the box.

2 Cover the surrounding area with newspaper when spray painting. Spray the lid with gold paint, applying it in thin coats. Allow the paint to dry between coats. Spray the box gold.

3 When dry, peel off the doilies. To remove any glue, wipe the surface with lighter fluid and a soft cloth. Tie gold ribbon around the box. Slip another length under the knot and fasten it in a bow. Cut the ends of the bow in chevrons.

Glitzy kitsch

Glitter paints are great fun to use. This wacky box has bold, glittery floral motifs and sparkling cabouchon jewel stones.

2 Glue a large jewel stone in the center of each flower outline. Glue small stones in the gaps between: they will form the center of smaller flowers.

You **will need . . .**

- Box
- Glitter paints
- Cabouchon jewel stones
- Acrylic gesso or latex paint
- Thin cardboard
- Craft paint
- All-purpose household glue
- Pencil
- Scissors
- Paintbrush

1 If you have a dark-colored box, use a paintbrush to apply an undercoat of acrylic gesso or latex paint. Leave to dry. Cut out simple flower shapes from thin cardboard to use as templates. Arrange the templates on the box and draw around them.

3 Working on one side of the box at a time, apply glitter paints to fill in the large flower shapes and create petals around the small jewel stones.

4 Draw stems and leaves with gold glitter paint in between the flowers.

5 Fill in the unpainted areas with silver glitter paint. Let it dry, then touch up any bare areas with more glitter paint.

Tortoiseshell book box

This smart tortoiseshell-effect book box would have pride of place in any library. Fake tortoiseshell was developed in the seventeenth century to meet the demand for the real thing and has remained a very popular paint technique.

You **will need ...**

- Book box
- Oil paint primer
- Yellow oil-based gloss paint
- Teak gloss varnish
- Oil paint in burnt umber and black
- Mineral spirits
- Polyurethane clear gloss varnish
- Decorator's brush
- Artist's paintbrush
- Tile or an old plate
- Black leatherette paper
- White glue
- Gold ribbon

1 Use a paintbrush to apply a coat of primer to the outside of the box, the edges of the underside of the "book covers," and a little over the spine of the book. Leave to dry. Apply two coats of yellow gloss paint. Allow to dry. Using a decorator's brush, apply teak varnish to one cover.

2 Use the decorator's brush to mark zigzags in the varnish, working diagonally from one corner to the other. Dab on large dots of teak varnish at random.

3 Dilute burnt umber and black oil paint with a little mineral spirits on a tile. With an artist's paintbrush, paint squiggles of burnt umber paint in the same direction as the diagonal zigzags. Paint smaller squiggles of black paint in the gaps.

4 Apply more teak varnish in the same direction as the zigzags. Apply another coat at right angles to the previous brushstrokes. Allow to dry. Decorate the other surfaces in the same way.

5 Apply a coat of clear gloss varnish. Set aside to dry. Cut a strip of leatherette paper to the width of the spine plus ⅜in (1cm). Use white glue to glue it to the spine, turning the ends over the edges. Cut and glue a rectangle of black leatherette paper to the underside of the cover.

Vintage
verdigris

Many metals corrode when the surface comes into contact with the air. Verdigris is the name of the resulting tarnished patination, and it can be reproduced easily with paints.

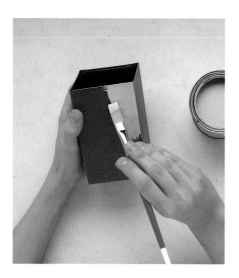

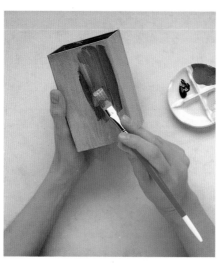

1 Cover the knob or handle with masking tape. Spray the box and lid with metal primer paint in a well-ventilated and protected area. Using a paintbrush, apply an undercoat of pale aquamarine latex paint to the box and let it dry.

2 Apply to the box and lid the two shades of aquamarine latex paint and the viridian gouache, blending the colors together.

3 Distress the surface by rubbing it gently with steel wool to reveal the undercoat, and even the metal in places.

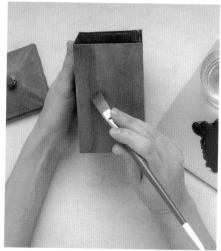

4 Apply a diluted coat of burnt
umber watercolor paint to give
an aged effect to the box and lid.
Let them dry, then remove the
masking tape. Apply two coats of
varnish to protect the surface. Twist
the end of an artificial sprig of ivy
around the knob or handle.

Very
fishy

Stenciling is a popular way of applying paint since professional results can be achieved so quickly. There is a huge selection of stencils.

You will need ...

- Wooden box
- Craft paints
- Stencil board
- Water-based satin varnish
- Flat paintbrush
- Stencil brush
- Masking tape
- Craft knife
- Cutting mat
- Tile or an old plate

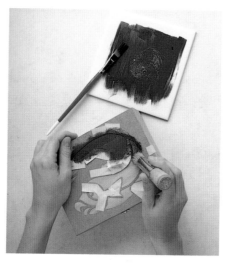

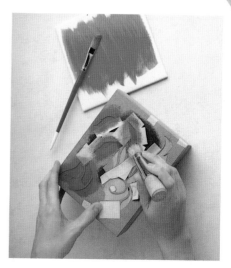

1 Apply paint thinned with water to the box to show the wood grain. Cut out the stencil using a craft knife on a cutting mat. Anchor the stencil to the box lid with masking tape. Apply masking tape around the first areas to be colored – in this case, the fish body – to protect the surrounding cutouts from paint.

2 Use a flat paintbrush to apply a thin film of paint to a tile or old plate. Holding the stencil brush upright, dab at the paint, taking care not to overload the brush. Apply the paint to the cutouts by keeping the brush upright and moving it in a circular motion. Let dry, then peel off the tape from the next cutouts.

3 Stencil the next color as before. When the paint is dry, stencil the remaining colors. Stencil some of the cutouts with gold paint to create highlights. Stencil smaller motifs on the sides of the box. To protect the surface, apply three coats of water-based varnish, allowing each coat to dry before applying the next.

Combed paint swirl

The simple technique of running a rubber comb over wet paint creates a striking pattern, enhanced by wavy lines and dots – an ancient and primitive design.

You will need ...

- Round plywood box 7in (18cm) diameter
- Water-based paint (any light color)
- Paintbrush
- Dark blue water-based paint
- Rubber comb
- Quick-drying acrylic varnish
- Varnish brush

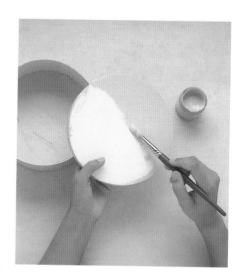

1 Apply two coats of light-colored water-based paint to the box and lid. Let the first coat dry before applying the next.

2 Brush the dark blue paint onto the lid. Immediately comb in the fan-shaped pattern. Comb a "flower" in the center. Apply blue paint on the side of the lid, and comb a wavy line into the paint.

3 Scratch wavy lines and dots in the panels as shown. Repeat on the sides of the box. Let it dry. Apply three coats of varnish.

Swish **fish**

This stylish box is made using a template. It is decorated with a stenciled and sponged effect, but could simply be spattered with paint.

2 Make the lid the same way. Line the joints with tissue paper applied with white glue.

You **will need . . .**

- Thin cardboard
- Scissors
- Glue gun
- Tissue paper
- White glue
- White latex paint
- String
- Poster paints in light green, dark green, blue, and orange
- Paintbrush
- Toothbrush
- Craft knife
- Small stencil brush
- Matte or spray varnish

Cardboard shapes for the box:
- 1 fish shape
- 2 equal, wide, rectangular side pieces
- 1 small, wide and folded rectangle for the tail

For the lid:
- 1 fish shape, as above
- 2 narrow equal side pieces
- 1 narrow, folded tail piece

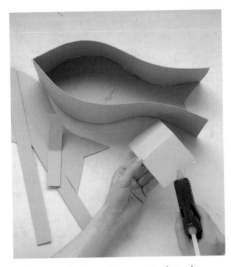

1 To make the box: use the glue gun to glue the two box side strips to one fish shape. Let them dry. Glue on the wide tail piece.

3 Apply a coat of latex paint inside and outside of the base and lid. Let it dry. If necessary, apply a second coat. Before the paint is dry, check that the lid fits. If the base is too wide, tie string around the tail area and leave overnight.

4 Apply light green paint to the box and lid. With a toothbrush, spatter with darker green. When dry, spatter with blue and orange.

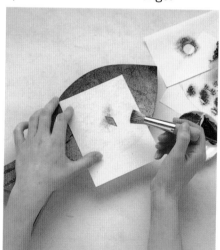

5 For further decoration, make simple paper stencils of various shapes. Mix a stiff consistency of both dark and light colors. Apply the light color using a small stencil brush. Sponge on the darker color. When dry, apply flat or spray varnish.

Rubber stamp
medley

A variety of rubber stamps is available from craft stores. Here, a combination of small linocuts, wooden type, and small steel engravings are used.

You **will need ...**

- Brown wrapping paper
- Round wooden box
- Scissors
- Stamps
- Oil-based linoleum inks – various colors
- Linoleum roller
- Wooden spoon
- Rubber glue
- Paintbrush
- Clear varnish

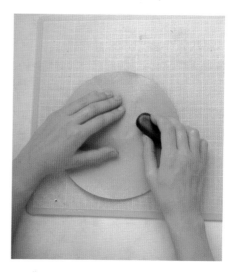

1 On a sheet of brown paper, carefully draw around the lid and cut out. Measure and cut out a long rectangle to cover the sides of the box exactly.

2 Squeeze a bit of oil-based linoleum ink onto a glass slab. Use the roller to distribute the ink evenly on the slab. Using the inked lino roller, ink up the stamps.

3 Place the brown paper on top of an inked stamp. Using a wooden spoon, rub the paper to transfer the ink from the stamp. To finish, use a paintbrush to apply glue to the box, then glue the back of the measured, printed brown paper to it. Coat with clear varnish.

4

Natural choice

The country is an endless source of inspiration for decorating with natural materials. Always be considerate of the environment. Collect only fallen leaves and flowers unless they are in your own yard. Craft stores and other specialist outlets supply dried flowers, colorful feathers, and shells.

Fragrance
of lavender

A delicate aroma of lavender from this pretty box will scent its surroundings. For a more intense fragrance, fill the box with potpourri and leave the lid ajar.

You **will need . . .**

- Colored wicker box
- Thick string or jute
- All-purpose household glue
- Scissors
- Lavender sprigs

1 Dab some glue onto one end of the string to prevent it from unraveling. When dry, cut diagonally across the glued end.

2 Coil the string into a close spiral and glue to one front corner of the lid. Arrange the string around the edge in a wavy pattern, with loops. Glue in place and cut off the excess string. Decorate the sides the same way.

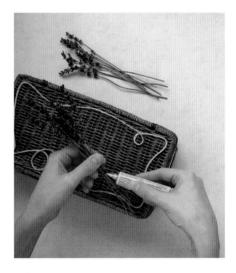

3 Arrange sprigs of lavender on the lid. Trim the ends if necessary, then apply glue to the lid and secure the flowers in position.

Beaded raffia box

The random method of weaving colored raffia on this funky mesh hatbox can be applied to any woven box. Shiny beads threaded onto the raffia add an interesting change of texture.

You **will need ...**

- Woven box
- Colored raffia
- Large-eyed needle
- Scissors
- Beads with large holes

1 Bunch raffia together in separate colors. Twist the lengths together. Wrap the twisted raffia around the lid rim and tie in a knot. Trim the trailing ends with scissors.

2 Thread a single length of raffia onto a needle. Fasten the end to the rim. Sew the twisted raffia to the rim with long diagonal stitches, threading on beads as you work.

3 Thread another single length of raffia. Thread it in and out of the mesh, threading a bead on each stitch. Tie the ends of the raffia to the mesh. Weave different-colored raffia in rows around the box. Leave space at the top for the lid.

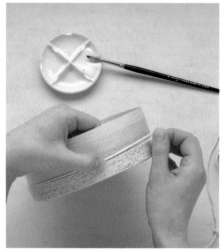

1 Apply a ½in (1.5cm) band of glue around the base of the box. Wind string tautly around the box, pushing it into position. Repeat until you reach the top.

2 To make a round decoration, cut a 7in (18cm) length of string, apply glue sparingly along its length, and wind it into a spiral. Glue the decorations evenly around the base.

String thing

String is easy to work with, and the decoration can be simple or complex. Colored string is readily available and contrasts well with natural colors. Incorporate bands of contrasting color for extra flair.

You **will need . . .**

- Wooden or cardboard box with lid
- White glue
- Paintbrush
- String in 3 colors
- Scissors
- Pencil
- Cardboard

3 To make the top tassel, wrap colored string around a 2½in (6.5cm) wide piece of cardboard 20 times and cut. Wrap string in a contrasting color around the cardboard 40 times and cut.

4 Carefully slip the string off the cardboard. Wind a small amount of string near the base and secure with a knot. Cut the folded ends to form a tassel and glue it to the center of the lid.

5 To make the front decoration, cut several 4in (10cm) lengths of string and secure with string around the middle, tied with a knot. Apply white glue and stick it to the contrasting string band.

Shell
box

Bright blue conjures up the sea and sky on a sunny day. Shells complement this idea and are used as feet for the box, attached to it with paper stuffing.

You **will need . . .**

- Rectangular box with lid
- Blue acrylic paint
- Paintbrush
- Shells in different sizes and colors
- White glue
- China glue

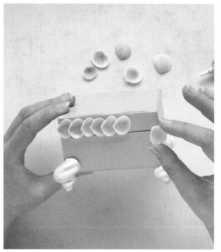

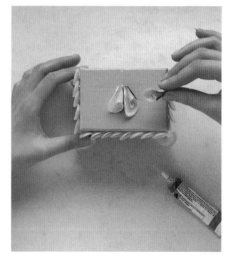

1 Using a paintbrush, coat the box with bright blue paint. Stuff paper into four big shells to use as feet for the box.

2 Apply white glue to the paper. Glue one shell to each corner of the box, matching the center point of the shells with the corners. Use china glue to stick shells onto the rim of the lid.

3 In the same way, glue more shells onto the center of the lid. Arrange the remaining shells and the small starfish in a pleasing design and glue in place.

Seaside **treasure**

Put vacation souvenirs to good use by decorating a straw box with seaside finds to evoke memories of happy excursions.

You **will need . . .**

- Straw box
- Broken fishing net
- Scissors
- Driftwood
- Seagull feathers
- Selection of shells, including a crab shell
- Glue gun or all-purpose household glue

1 Cut a section from a broken fishing net. Bunch it up and glue it to the center of the lid. An old net shopping bag could be used instead. Poke driftwood into the netting, pointing toward the corners. Glue in place.

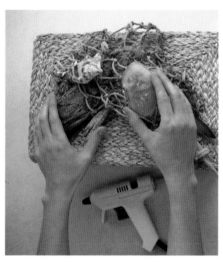

2 Glue a large shell and a crab shell on top of the net or use two large shells if you do not have a crab shell.

3 Glue more shells into the net and to the driftwood. Glue small shells to the lid. Glue small shells at random to the lid edges and box sides.

Spice is nice

This aromatic container is covered with spices and dried fruit slices. The cinnamon is trimmed in two different lengths to fit neatly.

You **will need . . .**

- Square or rectangular red cardboard box with separate lid
- Corrugated paper
- Peach-colored craft paint
- Cinnamon sticks
- Dried fruit slices
- Star anise
- Red loosely woven ribbon
- Red raffia
- All-purpose household glue
- Scissors
- Craft knife
- Paintbrush
- Ruler
- Pencil

1 Using a paintbrush, apply to the box peach-colored craft paint, diluted with water so the red box color shows through. Measure and cut a piece of corrugated paper to fit the lid. Apply household glue and stick in place.

2 Cut cinnamon sticks for the edges of the lid. Glue them in pairs to opposite edges, then to the remaining sides, as shown.

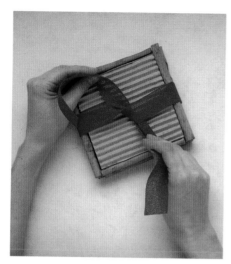

3 Using a dab of glue, attach the ends of two lengths of ribbon to the underside of the lid on opposite sides and tie a knot on top. Trim the ends of the ribbon diagonally.

4 Pierce the dried fruits and thread with raffia. Slip the raffia under the ribbon knot, tying it around three more short cinnamon sticks. Trim the ends and glue on a star anise.

Punch-work box

The wooden box with tin lid used here is available from craft or department stores. Keep your design simple for full effect.

1 Draw the design on paper. Use masking tape to secure it to the lid. Following the pattern, punch equally spaced holes with an awl through the paper into the metal lid. If the lid is thick metal, do the punching over the box. If it is thinner metal, punch onto a piece of softwood.

2 Work on the star and circles first, then punch the eight-pointed stars at each corner and in the center of the lid.

3 When the design is complete, peel off the paper to reveal the punched pattern.

Autumn leaves

A purchased recycled box with simple raffia decoration on the base was used for this project, but a plain shoe box is equally suitable. Pressed leaves are a colorful and cheap decorative material.

1 Leaves can be pressed at any time of the year, but the rich fall colors make the best selection. Lay the leaves between sheets of newsprint, weight down with books, and leave for three to four weeks. Smooth out leaves with a light iron set on medium.

2 Select some leaves in contrasting colors. Arrange them on the lid of the box, balancing the colors and overlapping some of the leaves. Use a paintbrush to apply glue to the underside of each leaf and press firmly into position. Let them dry.

3 Use a paintbrush to apply a coat of flat acrylic varnish for a natural look. Apply a spray varnish for a shiny finish.

Feather pompom

The "distressed" treatment of the paint creates an antique effect, and the feathers introduce an unusual three-dimensional aspect to the box surface.

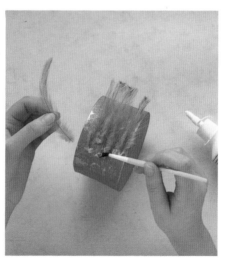

1 Apply gold paint to the box. When dry, apply the gray color over the gold and allow to dry. Rub the surface with sandpaper to reveal some of the gold color and achieve a speckled, antique effect.

2 Use a paintbrush to dot glue on the box. Attach each feather to the box by its base so that they overlap. Repeat the process on the rim of the lid.

3 The pompom: fold the ribbon in half lengthwise. Attach the feathers to it with loose stitches. Use the stitched yarn to pull the ribbon together to create the pompom. Secure with a knot. Glue it to the lid.

Pressed flower
bouquet

Pressed flowers on a gold background give this box a delicate richness. Make your own choice of flowers – White September and Chrysanthemum are used here.

You **will need . . .**

- Round wooden box
- White undercoat paint
- Paintbrush
- Gold powder
- Soft cloth
- Flowers of your choice
- Blotting paper
- Flower press
- Rubber glue
- Clear gloss varnish

1 Using a paintbrush, apply white undercoat to the wooden box and lid. Let it dry. Apply gold powder using a soft cloth, rubbing in small circles into the wood grain.

2 Pinch the stems off the flowers. Arrange them between sheets of blotting paper and place in a flower press. Secure the screws tightly. Leave the flowers in the press for at least two weeks, or longer if the flowers are large.

3 Carefully remove the flowers from the press and arrange them on the lid. Apply glue to the lid and apply the flowers. When dry, use a paintbrush to apply a coat of clear gloss varnish.

Fabulous fabric

From traditional boxes incorporating age-old sewing skills such as quilting to no-sew projects for the reluctant needleworker, this chapter presents a delightfully eclectic choice of boxes using a wide selection of fabrics and techniques.

Quilted **casket**

Design your own pattern to quilt by hand – a plain running stitch secures the three layers. The combination of velvet, taffeta, and quilting creates a look of luxury.

You **will need . . .**

- Oval or round shaped box with separate lid
- Dark red velvet
  6 x 5in (15 x 12cm)
- Lining material (cotton)
  6 x 5in (15 x 12cm)
- Filling material (batting or fiberfill)
  6 x 5in (15 x 12cm)
- Chalk
- Dark red sewing yarn
- White glue
- Dark red taffeta
  8 x 6in (20 x 15cm)
- Dark red string

1 Use the lid as a template to cut out pieces of velvet, lining, and batting, plus ¾in (2cm) allowance. Using chalk trimmed to a thin point, mark a simple pattern of quilting lines.

2 Pin together the velvet (with right side on top), batting, and lining. Sew plain running stitches along the marked pattern lines. Seal the quilt edges with white glue.

3 Glue the taffeta to the rim of the lid. Apply glue to the top of the lid and attach the quilt securely.

4 For a clean, decorative finish, twist dark red string and pin it on the velvet around the rim. Stitch in place. Seal the edges of the taffeta with glue. Apply glue around the base of the box and glue on the taffeta.

Sea chest

Silk moistened with water and glue is very soft and easy to form. Here it is manipulated to create a wave-like effect.

2 Cut the silk fabric in half. Moisten it with water. Using a paintbrush, cover the moist fabric with white glue.

You **will need . . .**

- Square or rectangular box with lid
- Blue acrylic paint
- Paintbrush
- Enough white silk organza to cover box and lid
- White glue
- Glass pearls in different sizes, transparent and blue
- China glue

1 Paint the box and lid bright blue. Let them dry.

3 Wind the glued fabric around the box, molding it into wave shapes as you go. Repeat steps 2 and 3 for the lid.

4 When the fabric is dry, use white glue to stick the pearls on the box and lid in an irregular design. Aim for a natural and organic effect.

5 Using china glue, glue transparent glass pearls as feet at each corner of the base of the box. Allow to dry thoroughly before standing the box upright.

1 Place the lid on paper and draw around it. Find a smaller circular object, place it in the center of the first circle, and draw around it. Find the center point, divide into equal parts, and design the star.

2 Cut out the separate segments. Place each one onto the fabric and draw around it, adding a ¼in (5mm) allowance. Cut out the shapes.

"French star" patchwork

Design your own pattern to recreate in patchwork. No sewing is involved – glue is used to secure the pieces. There are plenty of inexpensive books on patchwork full of other designs you could use.

You will need . . .

- Round box with lid
- Paper
- Pencil
- Ruler
- Small, sharp scissors
- Fabric pieces
- Paintbrush
- White glue
- Gold string

3 Apply white glue to the paper pattern segments. Fold the fabric edges over the paper shapes.

4 Clip the corners and trim the edges so the pieces lie flat. Use a paintbrush to apply glue to each piece. Glue the pieces to the lid, forming the design.

5 Apply glue to the side of the box and wind the gold string around it.

Pin-up in silk

This pretty gilded box decorated with silk and beads makes a perfect present for someone who does embroidery. Sawdust can be substituted for batting for a traditionally filled pincushion.

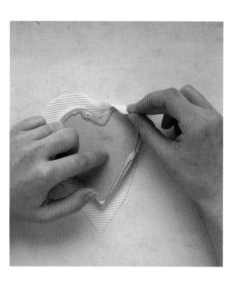

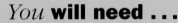

You **will need . . .**

- Wooden heart-shaped box with lid
- Varnish
- Metallic powders in gold and bronze
- Metallic paint medium
- Cardboard
- Scissors
- Batting
- Silk
- White glue
- Paintbrush
- Paper for stencil
- Stencil brush
- Straight pins
- Gold and pearl beads
- "Gold" charm

2 Make a cardboard template using the lid. Cut a heart from batting. Cut a silk heart ½in (13mm) larger. Put them together with the cardboard on top. Glue the edge of the cardboard and turn the silk over it.

1 Varnish the box and let it dry. Mix gold powder with the metallic medium. Apply with light brush strokes, a little at a time. Let it dry. Apply touches of the bronze color.

3 Cut out a smaller heart stencil and center it over the silk heart. Mix gold powder with metallic paint medium and lightly stencil the heart shape. Let it dry.

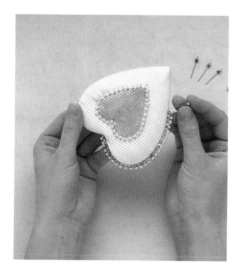

4 Pin pearl beads around the gold heart, and the gold charm in the center. Pin pearl and gold beads around the outside edge.

5 Apply a thin layer of white glue to the cardboard backing and place it in the center of the gilded lid. Press firmly. Let it dry.

You **will need . . .**

- Oval box with lid
- Medium-weight batting
- Latex glue
- Red and green slub fabric
- Straight pins
- Needlework scissors
- Thin cardboard
- Purple wire-edged ribbon 1½in (4cm) wide
- Pink ribbon ⅝in (1.5cm) wide
- Pink ribbon the width of the side of the lid
- Needle and thread
- Gold coin pendants
- Beads
- Large gold pendant

Echoes of Asia

This luxurious fabric-covered box is influenced by the rich colors of Asia. Gold coins and a glorious elephant motif complete the theme.

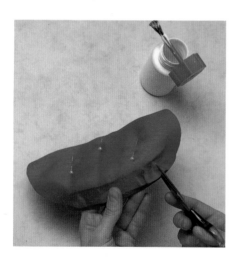

1 Cut an oval of batting to fit the lid and an oval of red fabric with a margin of ¾in (2cm) added. Glue the batting to the lid. Pin the fabric centrally on the batting. Glue the raw edges to the sides of the lid, clipping the fabric so that it lies flat.

2 Cut a strip of green fabric to fit around the box plus 1in (2.5cm). Glue one end in place. Wrap the strip around the box. Turn under the other end and glue sparingly. Glue the excess fabric to the base. Glue the fabric inside the top of the box.

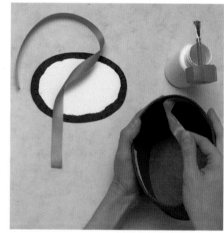

3 Cut an oval of thin cardboard ⅛in (3mm) smaller than the box base. Cover it with green fabric and glue it to the base inside the box. Glue narrow pink ribbon over the raw edges inside the box.

4 Pleat the purple ribbon. Make a small cut on each side. Knot a short length of ribbon at this point. Sew on a gold coin and a bead to the ends. Glue the loose ends inside the lid.

5 For the edge of the lid: sew a row of gold coins and beads to the pink ribbon. Glue it around the sides, finishing it neatly. Open the ribbon loops on top of the box. Sew a large gold pendant and a bead to the front of the box.

Tasseled **tapestry**

The sumptuous choice of fabric used to cover this box gives it a very regal look. The box is lined with a coordinating fabric, and a chunky tasseled cord adds a final touch of grandeur.

1 To cover the lid: cut enough tapestry fabric to cover the whole lid plus ⅜in (1cm) along each edge. Apply latex glue to the top and long sides of the lid. Glue the fabric to the lid. Fold under the fabric at the short sides, a neat fold at each corner. Mark the foldlines with pins.

2 Open out the fabric. Cut away the excess to within ⅝in (1.5cm) of the pins. Cut the fabric level with the edge of the lid. Refold and glue in place.

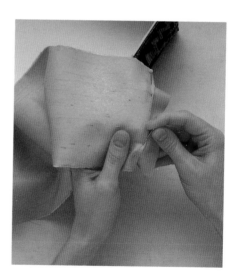

3 To make a lining for the lid: cut a strip of slub fabric measuring the total length of all the sides plus 4¾in (12cm). Its width measures the lid depth plus ¾in (2cm). Three-fourths of an inch (2cm) from one end of the strip, pin a pleat ⅜in (1cm) deep.

4 To glue the lining to the lid: apply glue to the inside edge of the top of the lid. With the pleat at one corner, glue one edge of the strip to the lid, laying it flat against the side. Continue to apply the strip, pleating it at each corner. Fold the end under. Glue in place.

6 Box lining: cut a strip of slub to cover the sides plus ¾in (2cm) all around. Follow step 4, omitting pleats. Glue the inside edges of the box. Press the fabric flat inside. Trim level. Cover the outside with slub, as in steps 1 and 2. Glue the raw edge inside the box.

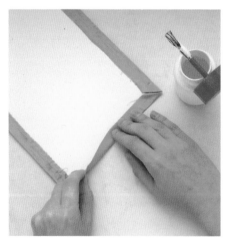

5 Pin the raw edge of the lining over the edge of the lid. Snip the corners so the fabric lies flat. Glue in place, leaving the edge raw.

7 To trim: glue lengths of braid over the raw fabric edges on both box and lid. Cover two rectangles of cardboard with slub. Turn the fabric under ⅜in (1cm) and glue. Glue the pieces inside the box and lid. Fasten with the cord.

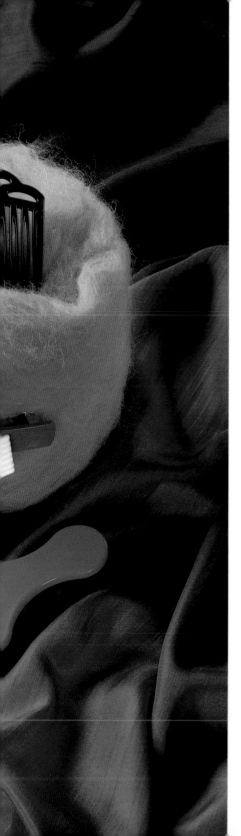

Wooly **box**

*Wool is a wonderfully textural material.
Try fur fabric as a variation.*

You **will need . . .**

- Round box with lid
- White glue
- Orange paint
- Golden-yellow wool fiber
- Paintbrush
- Glue brush

1 Paint the box and lid orange. Let them dry. Glue the wool fiber onto it.

2 Brush diluted white glue around the edges of the box to make a neat finish. Repeat on the lid.

1 Cut enough felt motifs and contrasting details to decorate the lid and box sides. Cut out a zig-zag design for the lid rim. Sew the details to the main felt shapes with single stitches. Highlight with random stitches.

Felt **good**

Stylized motifs cut from felt are sewn together with vibrant embroidery threads to trim this colorful box. A chunky bead is attached to the top as a practical knob to lift the lid.

You will need . . .

- Colored cardboard box with separate lid
- Colored felt
- Embroidery scissors
- Stranded embroidery floss
- Sewing needle
- Latex glue
- Heart-shaped beads
- Button
- Bead 1in (2.5cm) in diameter
- Bead ¼in (6mm) in diameter

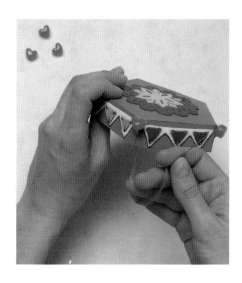

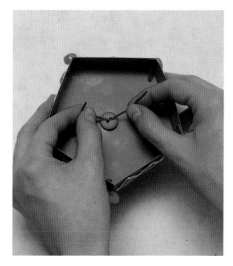

2 Glue the motifs and zigzags to the lid and box. Apply the glue sparingly so it does not seep through the fabric. Sew a heart-shaped bead at each corner of the lid. Fasten the thread ends inside.

3 To attach the knob: thread the needle through the button, then through the lid. Thread on the large bead, a heart-shaped bead, and the small bead. Insert the needle back through the beads, the lid, and out through the other button hole.

4 Tighten the thread so the beads sit one on top of each other. The button will act as a washer. Knot the thread ends securely together on the button.

6

Design in 3-D

Three-dimensional decorations are an ideal way to revamp an otherwise unusable box. A totally new look can be given to a box just by gluing on a pretty ornament – or you can go to the other extreme and create extravagant sculptural effects by building up the boxes with clay or salt dough.

Cake-deco **container**

Transform a plain box into this elegant classical building with the simple addition of a pair of cake-decorating columns and architectural details cut from mat board.

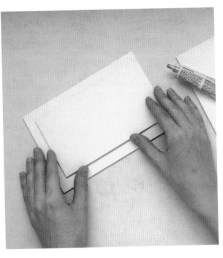

2 Glue the smaller pieces of cardboard on top and underneath the lid, in the center. Weight the lid with heavy books while the glue dries.

You **will need . . .**

- Lidless box, at least 5½in (13.5cm) high
- Two cake-decorating columns, each 3in (7.5cm) high
- Mat board (8-sheet thickness)
- Silver spray paint
- Pencil
- Craft knife
- Ruler
- Heavy books
- All-purpose household glue
- Paintbrush

1 To make the lid: on the mat board, lightly draw around the box base. Add ¼in (5mm) on all sides. Cut out using a ruler and craft knife. Cut two more pieces of mat board, ⅜in (1cm) smaller on all sides.

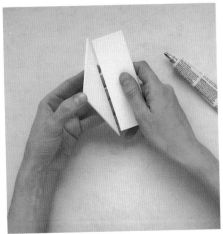

3 Glue the columns to the box 1¾in (4.5cm) apart. Cut mat board 4½ × 1½in (11.5 × 4cm). Cut a triangle: base 5in (12.5cm) long, sides 1½in (4cm) high. Glue them together on the long edges at right angles (90°).

4 Cut two equal triangles: bases 4⅛in (10.5cm), sides 1⅜in (3.5cm). Attach one triangle to the architrave as shown, for extra support. Glue the remaining triangle to the front.

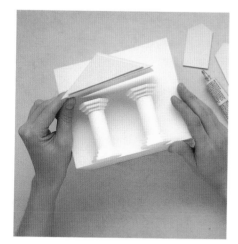

5 Glue the architrave on top of the pillars. Cut two simple window shapes and glue them to the box sides. Spray silver paint over the box and lid inside and out.

Salt-dough **sweetheart**

Salt dough is a traditional folk craft. The dough is modeled and then baked slowly in a home oven. This box is studded with twinkling glass jewel stones and painted with pearlized paints.

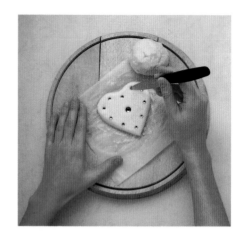

2 Arrange small jewel stones around the edges of the heart. Position a larger stone in the center. Embed the stones in the dough with the tip of a knife.

You **will need . . .**

- 6 tbsp. all-purpose flour
- 3 tbsp. salt
- 3 tbsp. water
- Bowl
- Airtight container
- Rolling pin
- Parchment paper
- Heart-shaped box
- Small knife
- Glass stones
- Fine sandpaper
- Wood glue
- Pearlized paints
- Paintbrushes
- Boat varnish

To make the salt dough, mix the flour, salt and half the water. Add the rest of the water, kneading the mixture into a pliable dough. Knead for another five minutes. Set aside in an airtight container for half an hour.

1 Roll out the dough ⅜in (1cm) thick on parchment paper. Using the box lid as a template, cut out a heart. Smooth the edge with a wet finger.

3 Roll 10 balls of dough ⅜in (1cm) in diameter and flatten each slightly. Bake all the dough pieces in an oven at 250°F for 6½ hours until the dough is completely hard. Turn off the heat and allow the pieces to cool in the oven.

4 Use sandpaper to smooth the edges and underside of the heart. Attach the heart to the lid and the balls to the rim with wood glue. Using a paintbrush, apply turquoise pearlized paint to the lid and box. Let them dry.

5 Paint details in contrasting colors of pearlized paint using a fine paintbrush. Apply six coats of boat varnish to the lid, allowing each coat to dry before applying the next, to protect the salt dough.
Note: It is important to keep salt dough away from moisture.

Golden finds

Densely embellished with exquisite buttons, jewels and baubles, this must be the ultimate jewelry box.

1 To make the handle, bend an ornate teaspoon into a suitable curved shape. You may need to secure one end of a metal spoon in a vice to bend it. The spoon here is a souvenir from a museum gift shop; it is made of plastic and therefore easy to bend. Glue a string of pearls around the lid circumference.

2 Arrange the materials on the lid in a pleasing design and glue them in place.

3 Fill in the areas between the decorations with gold relief paint and set aside to dry. Decorate the box and sides of the lid to match. Brush the box interior with mother-of-pearl acrylic paint.

Mosaic
magic

This colorful box is created using the ancient art of mosaic. Broken china and tiles are applied in a random, crazy-paved style around a central chunky ceramic knob.

You **will need ...**

- Old china and ceramic tiles
- Old towel
- Hammer
- Cardboard or wooden box with a separate lid
- Ceramic knob
- Ceramic tile adhesive and grout
- Adhesive and grout spreader
- Soft cloth

1 Wrap the china and the ceramic tiles in an old towel. Strike with a hammer to break into small pieces.

2 Glue a ceramic knob to the center of the lid with tile adhesive. Arrange the mosaic pieces on the lid in a random, crazy-paving pattern, leaving a gap of about ⅛in (3mm) between the pieces.

3 Apply tile adhesive, and cover the lid rim and box sides with mosaics. Allow a margin at the top of the box to fit the lid and a border of ¼in (5mm) for the grout. Wipe away excess adhesive. Let it dry.

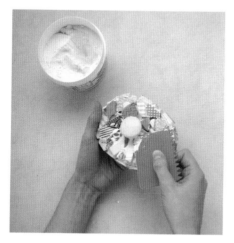

4 Spread grout over the ceramic pieces, filling the gaps. Wipe away excess grout with a damp cloth as you work. When the grout is completely dry, polish with a soft cloth.

Also **astrology**

Horoscopes hold a fascination for many people. This box, decorated with astrological symbols, has a star-sign motif modeled from clay on the lid.

You **will need . . .**

- Rectangular box with lid
- Air-drying clay
- Wooden cutting board
- Rolling pin
- Small pointed knife
- Superglue
- Acrylic gesso or latex paint
- India ink
- Paintbrushes
- Polyurethane flat varnish

1 Roll the clay out flat ¼in (6mm) thick on a wooden cutting board. Use the lid to cut a rectangle. Cut away the center, leaving a frame. Moisten the knife tip and pat the cut edges to smooth them. Divide the frame into "tiles".

2 Model a simple astrological motif from clay to fit within the frame. This water vessel represents Aquarius. Indent details with the knife tip. Set the clay pieces aside to harden overnight.

3 Glue the clay pieces to the box lid. Undercoat the box and lid with acrylic gesso or latex paint.

4 Paint the lid and box with India ink diluted with water. Paint astrological symbols on the box and sides of the lid. Apply two coats of varnish.

Celestial star

This heavenly container would make a delightful gift box for a special present. The silver-lined clouds are simple to apply using a natural sponge.

1 Using a paintbrush, apply an undercoat to the box and lid inside and out, using acrylic gesso or latex paint. When dry, paint with blue craft paint. Apply a thin film of white paint to a tile or old plate. Dab the paint with a small, damp natural sponge. Dab the sponge lightly onto the lid to suggest clouds.

2 When the "clouds" are dry, apply a thin film of silver paint to the tile or plate and dab with a clean, damp sponge. Dab the silver on the lower edge of the clouds. Let them dry and repeat with gold paint.

3 Glue an ornamental cherub to the top of the lid.

You will need . . .

- Oval box 5in (12.5cm) long
- Blue and green craft paints
- Old toothbrush
- Polymer clay, orange, green, and lemon yellow
- Parchment paper
- Rolling pin
- Small pointed knife
- Epoxy resin glue
- Water-based gloss varnish
- Paintbrush

1 Paint the lid and box blue. Paint the inside green. Lightly dab at the green paint with a toothbrush, then run a finger through the bristles to spatter the lid and box with paint. Let it dry.

Fruity beauty

Exotic fruits modeled from colored polymer clay are glued in bas-relief style to this quirky box. Experiment with making other fruits or even vegetables to glue to a practical kitchen storage box.

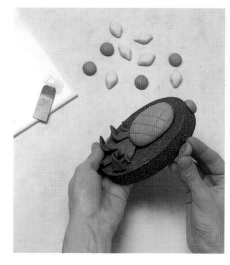

2 Draw around the lid on parchment paper. Roll a ball of orange clay 1¾in (4.5cm) in diameter. Mold to an oval for the pineapple. Flatten it slightly and place it on the parchment oval to size and position the design. Indent a crisscross design with the knife tip.

3 Roll out green clay flat ⅛in (3mm) thick. Cut pointed leaf shapes and position them, bending the leaf tips forward. Press the base of the leaves against the pineapple.

4 Roll balls of orange and yellow clay for the citrus fruits. Mold the yellow clay to form the lemons. Cut all the pieces in half, the lemons lengthwise. Reshape the fruits with your fingers. Bake, following the manufacturer's instructions. Let them cool. Glue the pineapple to the lid and the fruits to the rim. Varnish.

Copper
repoussé

The repoussé effect on this copper box is made by drawing with a dry ballpoint pen. Work on a soft surface so the marks can indent and create the relief.

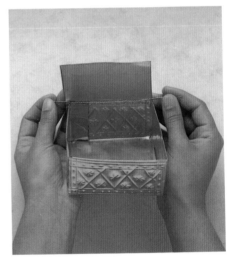

1 Mark the pattern of the box on the foil using a dry ballpoint pen and ruler. Use strong scissors to cut out the shape and small scissors to snip the fold-over tabs.

2 Lay the foil on a soft surface such as a magazine. Use a dry ballpoint pen and ruler to draw tramlines inside the panels of the box. Draw crisscross lines within each panel, and stars in the center of each diamond shape. Add dots into the tramlines.

3 Lay the tape on the edge of each side. Fold along the scored lines and draw each side up from the base. Fold the lining and tab over the decorated side. Press gently. Before folding the last side over, slip the copper wire into the fold, leaving 1¼in (3cm) at each end.

4 Mark the pattern for the lid slightly larger than the box and allow an extra ⅖in (1cm) all round.

5 Line the reverse of the lid, turning over the edges to secure it. Insert the wire into the folded section of the lid and twist the wire to join. To secure the hinge, fold the last edge over on the base of the box.

Delicious **box**

This appetizing confection is actually a round box with a clay "cream cake" modeled over the original lid. The box is deceptively simple to create, and the technique can be adapted to make all kinds of favorite pastries.

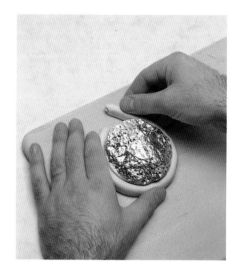

2 Squeeze a piece of baking foil into a dome. Glue it to the lid. Roll a "sausage" of clay ⅝in (1.5cm) thick. Slightly flatten it and wrap it around the lid.

You **will need . . .**

- Round box with separate lid
- Fine corrugated cardboard
- All-purpose household glue
- Pink and white craft paints
- Paintbrushes
- Baking foil
- Wooden cutting board
- Air-drying clay
- Craft knife
- Brown acrylic paint
- Red nail polish
- Puff paints

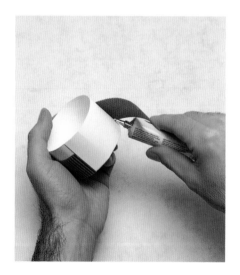

1 Cut a strip of corrugated cardboard long enough to wrap around the box, and to the height of the box with the lid on. Glue the strip around the box, even with the base. Paint the box pink.

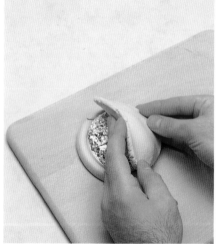

3 Roll a ball of clay and flatten it between your fingers to a circle ¼in (6mm) thick for the icing. Place the icing over the foil and press onto the pastry. Smooth over the surface of the icing with moistened fingers.

4 Roll a ¾in (2cm) diameter ball of clay for a cherry. Make a dent in it with a paintbrush. Make a depression in the top of the icing. Press in the cherry.

5 Set the clay cake aside to harden. Pull out the original lid. Dilute brown acrylic paint and paint the pastry. Paint the icing white, and the cherry with nail polish. Dot puff paint on the icing.

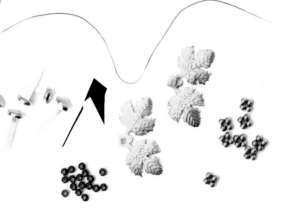

Eggstrordinary **fabergé**

This simple egg requires very little skill. It looks ornate, but is easy to make. The cardboard egg boxes can be bought at Easter from toy, stationery, or gift stores. There is a vast array of beads and sequins available.

You **will need . . .**

- Cardboard Easter egg
- Enamel silver spray paint
- Paper fasteners
- Selection of gold and colored glass beads, leaves, etc.
- Jewelry glue
- Gold jewelry wire
- Sharp nails or scissors

1 Spray the cardboard egg inside and out with silver enamel paint. Let it dry. Make an incision with a sharp point at both ends of the egg and on the sides. Insert the paper fasteners.

2 Glue the leaves around the rim. Decorate the paper fasteners with beads, using glue to secure them. Glue four small beads onto the base of the box to allow it to stand upright.

3 Cut three pieces of wire, one the length of the egg and two twice the length. Fold in half. Decorate with pearls and beads. Twist the wire pieces around each other.

4 Secure two wires across the egg using the paper fasteners. Finish with the longer piece from one end of the egg to the other. Decorate the top with threaded beads and leaves. The base is decorated with twisted wire fastened onto paper fasteners at each end.

Glossary

This comprehensive list of definitions is useful to refer to if you come across unfamiliar terms in the projects.

Acrylic gesso
A thick, creamy substance used as an undercoat, often under gilding. Gesso can be bought at art supply stores.

Acrylic matte medium
This versatile medium can be used as a varnish, or mixed with gold powder to brush onto a wooden surface.

Acrylic paint
A popular artist's paint that is water soluble when wet but water resistant when dry. Available in a wide choice of colors from art supply stores, the paint dries quickly to a flat finish.

Air-drying clay
A self-hardening modeling clay that dries on contact with the air. Keep the clay in an airtight container when not in use and moisten it with water while you are modeling it.

Antique varnish
Also called aging varnish. This tinted medium can be brushed onto a decorated box to darken the surface subtly. Refer to the manufacturer's instructions for cleaning brushes and drying times.

Awl
A woodworking tool with a metal point that is used to make holes.

Cabouchon jewelry stones
Colored glass jewelry stones with flat backs for gluing.

Copper foil
Fine-gauge metal that can be cut with scissors (use an old pair as the metal will blunt the blades). The foil is thin enough to be folded and embossed.

Crackle varnish
A preparation that gives a cracked, transparent effect. This is achieved by applying a quick-drying medium over a slow-drying one, causing cracks to appear in the top layer. Emphasize the cracks by rubbing in oil paint.

Craft knife
A craft knife or scalpel is indispensable for craftwork. Use on a cutting mat to cut smoothly through paper and cardboard. Replace the blades often. Do not attempt to cut right through thick cardboard or mat board at the first approach; instead, cut several times gradually deeper.

Craft paint
A non-toxic quick-drying paint that is usually acrylic-based. Craft paints are available at art and craft stores in a large choice of colors and finishes, including pearl, metallic, flat, and glossy.

Cutting mat
A plastic mat available at art and large stationery stores. Use a cutting mat when cutting with a craft knife or scalpel. The surface is self-healing so can be used again and again and is slower to blunt blades than other surfaces.

Escutcheon pins
Fine brass pins that will not split wood when hammered in.

Glitter paint
Colorful plastic particles are suspended in a glue that dries transparent so only the glitter is visible. Glitter paint can be brushed on, but is usually squeezed from a tube through a fine nozzle.

Gold powder
Metallic powder made from finely powdered bronze that can be applied with a finger or cloth, or mixed with another medium and brushed on.

Gouache
A water-based tube paint that is water-soluble when dry. Gouache is thicker and more opaque than watercolor or acrylic paint.

India ink
Available in small jars from art supply stores, India ink can be thinned with water and applied as a wash.

Latex paint
Opaque water-based household paint that can also be used as an undercoat for many other paint finishes.

Linoleum roller
A small roller to roll over rubber stamps or découpaged papers to ensure even coverage.

Masking tape
A low-tack tape that is useful for sticking motifs temporarily in place when arranging them. Always use a very low-tack masking tape and check that it will not mark or tear your material before use.

Mat board
Thick board made of layers of paper. Available at art and picture-framing stores in various thicknesses. Mat board is traditionally used to make borders or mats for pictures, but is also useful for making shapes to add to boxes.

Oil paints
Artist's oil paints are available in tubes from art stores and can be thinned with mineral spirits. The paints are slow-drying, and brushes must be cleaned with mineral spirits.

Paper ribbon
Often used in gift wrapping and flower arranging, paper ribbon is a strip of randomly creased paper that comes in the form of a twisted rope.

Plastic putty
A soft putty-like substance that will not harden. It will adhere to most surfaces, so it can be used to hold decorations temporarily in place while you are arranging them.

Polymer clay
A popular modeling material that can be bought at art, craft, and toy stores. The clay comes in a choice of colors that can be blended together; always wash your hands between colors. The clay is baked in an oven and can be varnished afterward.

Primer
This term describes any substance that is applied to a surface in preparation for painting. Always use a primer suitable for the type of paint you are using.

PVA medium
PVA stands for polyvinyl acetate. This multipurpose glue is white when wet and transparent when dry. PVA medium has been used for many of the projects in this book. It can be thinned with water and used as an adhesive and for making papier-mâché.

Relief paint
A thick, creamy paint that comes in a tube or bottle with a fine nozzle to distribute the paint and dries standing above the surface.

Salt dough
A modeling material made from plain flour, salt, and water. Salt dough is baked slowly in a cool oven to harden it. The finished model must have many coats of varnish applied and be kept in a dry atmosphere.

Sealant
A solution painted onto a surface to prevent it from affecting the decoration that is applied to it. Sanding sealer is a versatile sealer which can be used on wooden boxes and applied to thin papers to prepare them for découpage.

Stencil board
A hard-wearing waxed cardboard used to make stencils.

Stencil brush
This brush has short, thick bristles. Hold the brush upright when stenciling and move it in a circular motion to distribute the paint.

Varnish
It is advisable to varnish most completed boxes for protection. Choose a varnish suited to the finish of the box. Water- and acrylic-based varnishes dry quickly to a clear finish. Polyurethane varnishes are slower to dry and will yellow the surface slightly but are very hard-wearing. Always varnish in a dust-free area and use a good-quality flat brush, ideally a badger-hair varnishing brush. Clean brushes immediately after use.

Index

Page numbers in *italics*
refer to illustrations

Cheryl Owen designed and made:
Safari stripes, Checkered tissue, Fabric découpage, Glitzy kitsch, Very fishy,
Seaside treasure, Celestial star, Golden finds, Fragrance of lavender, Salt-dough sweetheart,
Mosaic magic, Marquetry magic, Tortoiseshell book box, Vintage verdigris,
Tasseled tapestry, Cake-deco container, Spice is nice, Also astrology, Fruity beauty,
Felt good, Delicious box, Lovely lace, Beaded raffia box, Echoes of Asia.

Carol Wilhide designed and made:
Pressed flower bouquet, Rubber stamp medley, Garden collage, Stamps galore,
Weaving spells, World in a box, Alphabet set.

Daniela Zimmermann designed and made:
Sea chest, Shell box, "French star" patchwork, Feather pompom, Quilted casket,
Wooly box.

Deborah Schneebeli-Morrell designed and made:
Day of the dead, Punched-work box, Combed paint swirl, Découpage in flower,
Copper repoussé box.

Gill Dickinson designed and made:
Child's elebox, Pin-up in silk, String thing, Cactus pencil box, Swish fish, Autumn leaves,
Eggstrordinary Fabergé, Bowtie box.

The publisher would like to thank Mill Store Products Inc., New Bedford, Massachusetts,
for providing blank boxes free of charge.